A BUNCH OF SWEET PEAS

A BUNCH OF
SWEET PEAS

HENRY DONALD

Illustrated by Ann Ross Paterson

CANONGATE

A VILLAGE MANSE

On the twentieth of February, in the year nineteen-eleven, Lord Northcliffe's halfpenny newspaper, the *Daily Mail*, announced a new competition.

A prize, the paper stated, of one thousand pounds would be offered for the best bunch of sweet peas grown by an amateur gardener anywhere in the British Isles.

Second and third prizes of £100 and £50 would also be awarded, as well as one hundred silver medals and nine hundred bronze medals.

The announcement of the competition caused a sensation. A thousand pounds, in those days, represented a small fortune. Gardening was a popular hobby, even more widespread than it is now. Horticultural societies flourished everywhere; shows were regularly held; and people competed eagerly for nothing more valuable than coloured cards, indicating a first, second or third. Nothing like the *Daily Mail's* lavish proposals, in that Coronation Year of 1911, had ever been heard of.

In the Scottish Border village of Sprouston, young Alec White, who had begun to earn his living by gardening, read about the competition and made a mental note of it.

Sprouston was just a little place, close by the south bank of the River Tweed, a few miles downstream from Kelso. There was a village green, two or three rows of cottages, and a plain square church sitting on top of an ancient grassy mound.

Just below the church, in one of the thatched cottages, was the combined shop and post-office, where Miss Jemima Ross sold, amongst other things, paraffin for the lamps, bundles of sticks for the fire, sweeties in glistening jars for the children, and in the corner, next to the ivy-bordered window where the letter-box was, stamps and postal-orders. If anyone was in a hurry Mima Ross could even send telegrams to the general post-office at Kelso, or of course receive them.

Opposite Mima's shop, on the other side of the road, and sheltered by a pink stone wall, was the Manse. The garden of the Manse was one of the places where Alec White worked. So it was young Alec who, on that February day in 1911, told the parish minister of Sprouston, Mr Denholm Fraser, about the *Daily Mail* sweet pea competition.

Denholm Fraser was a tall spare man, in his thirties, who wore the sober garb and white collar of his calling.

He was married to a charming and pretty wife, and they had a little daughter of five. Brought up in a Highland Manse himself, Mr Fraser was accustomed to economy. At Edinburgh University he had got himself through the Divinity Hall on a bursary of £32 a year and by tutoring three or four hours a day. When he became an assistant at the Tron Kirk in Edinburgh he decided it would be best to live down near the Cowgate in one of the slum tenements. It is said that with his steady quiet manner, Denholm Fraser won the respect and trust of the poorer people of the parish. He also learned, climbing the dark crowded tenement stair, what real poverty meant. So when, before his marriage, he was chosen to be the minister of Sprouston, the smallness of his yearly stipend there did not unduly worry him.

It was while he was in Edinburgh that he met the future Mrs Fraser, who lived on the sunny South Side of the town. Two years after his appointment to Sprouston they were married, and he brought her to live at the Manse.

It took the young bride some time to get used to living in quite such a remote out-of-the-way place. At

first Mrs Fraser missed her Edinburgh girlhood, with its dances and concerts and dinner-parties, the busy shops in Princes Street, and all her friends. But by 1911, with her five-year-old daughter to look after, she had settled down.

The village, with its little church, the broad tidy fields round about, the peaceful river flowing by—all seemed to have caught her in some country spell. Shy and reserved when she first came, the minister's wife had learned how to break through the canny Border reserve of the village folk. She presided at Mothers' Meetings; she busied herself with the Sunday School, and with her training in music taught the children to sing. Much to her own surprise, Mrs Fraser had gradually discovered that this was, somehow, just the sort of life she was made for.

Mr Fraser had also made a discovery. Now that he had a garden of his own, he found that he not only liked gardening but that he had a gift for it. He began learning from Alec White, and whenever he had time to spare from the various duties of the parish, he would cross the grassy lawn in front of the house and go down into the old walled garden beyond, to weed and dig, prune and stake and tie, and also, of course, when the warm weather came, to cut.

It was when the flowers were cut and brought indoors that Mrs Fraser took an interest in them. The house, not yet completely furnished, was her province. It was a neat compact house, with three rooms on the ground floor, the study and the bedrooms up the steep curving staircase, and the kitchen premises at the back. By now, she had grown very fond of her new home. It was, she thought, just the place to bring up a family. The only trouble was that it still needed so much doing to it. Inside, the house looked shabby and bare. And this used to worry her, because she hadn't yet grown accustomed to being so poor. On the one hand she had all sorts of ideas about carpets and tables and chairs, chintz-covers and curtains, and on the other she had to count every penny just to keep things going as they were.

But she was happy. They were both happy. Of course, they didn't know then that they were going to stay at Sprouston Manse for another twenty-eight years, that there would be four daughters altogether,

and that when the two wars were over, they would find a quiet resting-place at last close by the little church they had served so faithfully their whole lives long. They didn't know it that far-off February day in 1911, when young Alec White was telling Mr Fraser about the Sweet Pea Competition.

At first Mr Fraser wasn't keen on the idea. Not that

the sweet peas which he had grown for the first time the previous year weren't very promising. But what hope could there possibly be for flowers that would have to be sent by rail all the way from Scotland to London? Before the 400-mile journey was over they would be withered.

'We wouldn't have a chance, Alec,' he said. No, no, better to send them to the Kelso Society Show. They had already won a card or two for their carnations; they would try the sweet peas at Kelso.

But young Alec was nothing if not determined. He knew good flowers when he saw them. As a'body kenned, he insisted, sweet peas travelled well. Besides, the soil where the Manse sweet peas had been grown was of first rate quality. 'Ye'll mebbe', he told Mr Fraser, 'ye'll mebbe win a medal!'

And so, eventually, Mr Fraser gave in. After all, it wasn't entirely outside the bounds of possibility that they might be awarded one of the bronze medals the paper was offering. He could put it on the mantelpiece in the study, beside the cards he had won at Kelso.

The sweet peas he had planted the year before had been something of an experiment. A new book on the subject had recently been published, and Mr Fraser had carefully followed the author's recommendations. He had put the plants in the kitchen-garden behind the house, where the soil was rich and dark and alluvial, washed into place long ages before by a wider more

turbulent Tweed. The plants had come up well, but now, as Alec pointed out, if they were going to raise prize blooms good enough to win a bronze medal, they must set about the business more thoroughly.

So the two twenty-yard trenches they dug at the end of February were wide and deep, six feet wide and four and a half feet deep, right down to the ancient gravel bed of the river. The bottom of the trenches was then lined with sackfuls of old leaves, and a load of steaming cattle-manure, carted down from one of the Sprouston farms, was mixed in with the soil.

In March, with a dusting of lime and a sprinkle of superphosphate, the plants were put in. The plants came from the greenhouse. Some had been sown in the previous September, some in January.

Now in the shelter of the kitchen-garden, the little seedlings began to reach down exploratory roots into the dark richness below.

BUSINESS MATTERS

The conditions for sending an entry to the *Daily Mail* Sweet Pea Competition of 1911—frequently listed, as the days passed, in successive editions of the paper— were surprisingly simple. If you were an amateur gardener who didn't employ more than one man to help, you could compete. You could send in one bunch only, but any member of your family could also send a bunch. Each entry was to be made up of twelve spikes or sprays, consisting of not fewer than three different varieties. There was no entrance fee. You didn't even have to be a regular reader of the paper.

The enthusiasm aroused by the competition extended, naturally enough, to seed-merchants. Nothing like £1000 had ever been offered for a bunch of flowers before, and the additional prizes of £100 for the second best and £50 for the third, not to mention the medals, ensured that the number of competitors would be enormous.

'I foresee,' the head of one London firm optimistically declared to a *Daily Mail* reporter, 'I foresee that we ourselves shall sell over twenty tons of sweet-pea seed.'

In Reading, in Manchester, Liverpool, Birmingham, Newcastle, and all over the north of England, the demand for seeds broke all records. A well-known St Albans firm offered a supplementary prize of £100 if the thousand-pound bunch was grown from a packet of their seeds. And then, in March, a famine in soot suddenly developed. Soot was an effective manure and insect-repeller. Everybody was laying in stocks of it.

By the middle of March the *Daily Mail* committee appointed to organise the scheme came to the conclusion that the only building in or near London large enough to display all the entries, for the purpose of judging them, would be the Crystal Palace. They accordingly decided that the show would be held there on the 28th and 29th of July. There might be, they thought, as many as ten or fifteen thousand bunches, or even more.

One sweet-pea specialist in Cambridge pooh-poohed the whole idea and stated in public that he was prepared to name the winner of the thousand-pound prize in advance.

'There are some growers,' he said, 'who not only make a habit of the culture, but who are pot-hunters, and the prize will go to one of these.'

Meantime, away in the north, in Sprouston, Mr and Mrs Fraser paid no attention to all this excitement, except of course to joke, as people who enter for competitions will, about what they would do when *they* won the thousand-pound prize. There really wasn't time, as the weeks hurried by and the spring came. Kirk Session meetings, Presbytery meetings, sermons to write, young communicants to instruct, schools to inspect, the sick or bereaved to be visited and helped, baptisms, marriages, funerals.

And besides all that, there was an addition to the family at the Manse. Mrs Fraser's second daughter was born.

But the sweet peas were not neglected. Poles eighteen feet long were planted at intervals along the trenches; wire was stretched between them; and then

dead branches woven between the wires. And now, as the spring of 1911 suddenly ripened into an early summer, the pale green shoots began to creep up the branches; delicate tendrils caught at the wire and curled to grip it; and soon the plants, thick and healthy, were shoulder-high. With the gardening skill he had now acquired, and an occasional word of advice from Alec, Mr Fraser carefully tended the plants, nipping and pruning and tying.

He had time to think as he stood there, working away, and one of the matters that occupied his mind, in that year, was the alteration he wanted to make in his church. For inside, the little church at Sprouston was like a square box. He wanted to ease its Calvinistic plainness and severity. Mr Fraser's plan was to build a chancel on to the end of it.

Nothing elaborate, of course. Just an arch, and a couple of steps, leading up; and then a window, perhaps, and a table below it—a table where newly picked flowers might be arranged each Sunday: say, a bunch of sweet peas.

Some money had been collected already, but not nearly enough. There was no doubt that if he were in a position to make a really substantial contribution, a really big sum—like fifty pounds—there might be more chance of gradually begging the rest.

Fifty pounds might just do it.

By June a ladder was needed, for in those days the method of cultivation was to let the plants grow as high as they would. And now the first buds appeared. Alec was full of invention. A cow had been temporarily installed in the Manse byre at that time, and Alec allowed nothing that fell to the stone floor of the byre to be wasted. Pailfuls of material were transformed, by the admixture of water from the garden tap, into pungent aromatic liquors, which he then poured into the thirsty roots of the sweet peas. A lot of water was needed because of the shortage of rain. But the first blooms that were brought into the house were magnificent: pink and violet, red and purple. They were better than last year's.

Naturally, Mrs Fraser, as she arranged them and drank in their perfume, couldn't help dreaming.

Of course, it was silly even to think of winning the *first* prize. With fifteen thousand entries it was probably silly to think of winning even a medal. But just supposing the impossible happened. What could she not do to her house with fifty pounds to spend?

Or even a hundred. *A hundred pounds!*

And then the drought came.

WEATHER REPORT

The drought, noted each day in the newspapers, had been threatening all through June. Now, with July, it started in real earnest. The whole of Great Britain was affected. In the first week of July, according to the country-wide meteorological reports, the drought was total.

At Sprouston Manse steps were taken to make up for the lack of rain. The squeaky hand-pump at the bottom of the flower-garden was in constant use, drawing up cool spring water from its hidden reservoir. But as the second week passed in an unrelieved glare of hostile sunshine, the tall climbing plants began to suffer. They were beginning to dry up. No amount of water applied to their roots could save them. What was needed was shade, and soft gentle rain to moisten not only the roots but the leaves and buds, to lie in glistening diamonds in the corners of all that tangled tracery of green.

Day after brilliant day went by, but no rain came.

By the morning of July 14th the prospects suddenly seemed hopeless. As the entries to the competition had to be received at the Crystal Palace by parcel post on Thursday, July 27th, ready for the judging on the 28th, they would have to be dispatched on Wednesday the 26th. The Sprouston sweet peas would therefore have to be picked, and packed, not later than the 25th. Unless it rained, they could not possibly survive the

28

long journey and at least thirty-six hours without water. But the forecast in the *Scotsman* newspaper on July 14th held out no possibility of change. The anticyclone covering the whole country, it reported, was stationary. The drought, now approaching a record duration, would continue.

Mr Fraser and Alec had done everything they could. All side shoots had been nipped off, and each plant was allowed to bear only from one to three stems. In the middle of the first scorching week of July the plants had been systematically disbudded in order to give them a rest. Now, in the last vital ten days, everything depended on rain and some relief from the burning sun. Otherwise, there would be no point in sending an entry at all. There would be no bronze medal, let alone anything so improbable as a prize.

But it was on that very day, July 14th, as the papers later admitted, that something happened. A small depression made an unexpected and completely un-heralded appearance just to the east of Iceland.

Skirting the coast of Scandinavia, the depression first travelled in a southerly direction, and then, influenced by some unknown cause, it turned west and edged towards the north of Great Britain.

Slowly, fractionally, the vast solid bulk of the anti-cyclone began to shift. A narrow corridor was formed, just wide enough to admit a blanket of cool rain-bearing cloud from the sea.

It didn't last long that first day: perhaps the length of the afternoon. But, as the meteorological records show, between Coldstream and Kelso, almost a tenth of an inch of rain fell.

It was the sign that Mr Fraser and Alec had been waiting for. There was still hope. They laid down more soot, more fertiliser, a careful dose of nitrate of soda. They watered it all in with pail after pail from the groaning pump.

The next day the sun came out again, but the weather was clearly unsettled. On the 17th there was another shower; on the 19th it rained again. On the 20th, just as the new flowers were beginning to open, it rained heavily; there was another tenth of an inch on the 21st.

And then, on the 22nd, as the silver drops slid and fell from stalk and leaf and tendril, the sun, tempered now by the moist air, beamed forth once more. It was just what the new flowers needed. You could almost believe—if you wanted to—that the whole operation had been carefully planned. At precisely the right moment, the drought, in the Borders, had broken.

Mr Fraser had left nothing to chance. He had sent in his entry forms at the appointed time. He had picked bunches of the separate varieties of sweet peas, packed them in cardboard boxes with moss, or sawdust, or cotton-wool, or in greaseproof paper; left them out all night and half the next day, just as if they really had been posted; and then unpacked them again, to see how they had survived. By Tuesday, July the 25th, when in the cool of the evening he walked down to the kitchen-garden to cut his flowers, he knew just what he was going to do.

He cut two bunches, each of twelve spikes, as the rules of the competition laid down; not too full blown, nor yet too tender; but blooms that in two days' time would reach their pitch of perfection. And when he had chosen them, carefully matching the colours, he brought them, a bunch in either hand, into the drawing-room of the Manse, where Mrs Fraser was sitting.

He explained to her that the rules permitted that an entry could be sent by each member of a family. Therefore he thought they would send in two bunches, one from her and one from himself. So he wondered if she would like to choose the bunch that would be entered under her name. And he held them up for her to see.

They were beautiful.

In one hand, he held a riot of passionate colour: glowing pink and flaming crimson, carmine and darkest purple. And in the other, in complete contrast, shades of the most exquisite feminine delicacy: pale lilac, the faintest rose, pure white. On each stalk there were four blooms, some of them more than two inches across. The stalks themselves, ribbed and fluted and curved, were nearly eighteen inches long.

And Mrs Fraser said, 'Oh, no, Denholm. *You* must choose. After all, they're your sweet peas. You must decide which you think the best.'

She remembered afterwards how he hesitated, glancing from one hand to the other. And then, indicating the delicate bunch, with its calm serene colouring, he said, 'I choose these'.

'All right,' said Mrs Fraser. 'Then I'll send in the others.'

The flowers were put in water, and some time that night they were packed. First the stalks of each bunch had to be tied with a special label, bearing a number which corresponded with the number on the entry form. On one of the two entry forms which he had sent off, Mr Fraser had written 'Mrs J. H. Fraser'—her own initials—and on the other his own name. (No names were to be revealed, of course, until the judging was over. Every entry with its numbered label was anonymous.)

Each of the two bunches was now wrapped in grease-proof paper, and then carefully surrounded in its separate box with a cushion of cotton-wool. The boxes were closed, tied up, and printed labels, addressed to the Sweet Pea Competition at the Crystal Palace, attached on the outside.

They were ready.

On the morning of Wednesday, July 26th, Mr Fraser got up early, and at six o'clock he set off alone on his bicycle, with the two boxes strapped to the carrier, to ride to the general post-office at Kelso. From cottage windows they saw him go. By this time, of course, the whole village knew. If they didn't know, they only had to ask Mima Ross. Being so close to the Manse, she had been hearing day by day how the sweet peas were progressing.

Mr Fraser was back by breakfast time, and already the inevitable reaction had set in.

'Well, Nettie,' he said to Mrs Fraser, as he sat down, 'that's the last we'll hear of those!'

It did seem, as he looked back, rather a waste of time and energy. There were amateur gardeners all over the south of England, as the specialist had said, comfortably off landed gentry, who had been growing sweet peas for years. Whereas this was only his and Alec's second crop. There was only one thing to do: forget all about it.

He would have to think up a more practical scheme for collecting money for the chancel. If the chancel ever was to be built. Perhaps it was just a dream that would never come true.

And Mrs Fraser began to think, as she had sometimes done in the early days, that perhaps they would have to go somewhere else. Instead of improving, the stipend, fluctuating with the teinds, was growing less. They simply couldn't go on like this—not as things were now.

Could it really be that they were *meant* to leave? To leave Sprouston?

DREAMS AND REALITY

Had Mr and Mrs Fraser known what was happening at the Crystal Palace in far-away London on that and the following day, they would have realized just how remotely improbable their dreams had become.

As the official labels had only been issued in return for a properly filled up application form, the organisers now knew how many bunches to expect. Five days before the show, the Post Office and the Railway Companies were advised of the alarming situation, and asked to take steps to avoid a total breakdown. Some-how, between 6.00 a.m. and 9.00 p.m. on Thursday, July 27th, all the boxes of blooms had to be delivered through the post to the Crystal Palace, so that they could be immediately unpacked and ready for the final judging on the Friday morning.

But the previous assessment of the number of competitors, the organisers discovered, had been wildly underestimated. The number of boxes they now expected to receive might be as high as 40,000.

A 300-foot marquee was put up at the goods entrance to the Crystal Palace, and two rows of tables were arranged along its entire length. Five hundred Boy Scouts, with Scout Masters to preserve discipline, were accommodated in tents near by.

On the morning of Thursday the 27th all was prepared, and the carefully planned routine swung into action. As the red post-office vans clip-clopped up to the entrance, parties of Scouts were waiting to unload them. The sacks of boxes were carried into the marquee and placed on the first row of tables. There, another party of Scouts unpacked them and carried each bunch to the second row of tables, where the preliminary judges were sitting.

This was the first fatal test. If the flowers were considered of sufficient merit to compete at all, they were arranged by the judge in one of the vases of water beside him. If not, they were rejected. As it turned out, in the course of the day a total of approximately 38,000 bunches was received. Of these, more than half never even got past the marquee.

The vases of chosen flowers were then conveyed on trollies by a third squad of Scouts into the Main Hall of the Crystal Palace. Here more tables had been set up, and two further committees of judges were in attendance. Their task was to select the two or three thousand bunches from which the medal and prize winners would be chosen.

The work went on all day. Night fell, and still the wagons rolled in. The tireless Scouts and judges worked on hour after hour. It wasn't until Friday morning dawned that every bunch had been received, unpacked, rejected or accepted, arranged in water, taken into the Main Hall, and there either left where it stood, or carried to the special tables. By Friday morning there were two and a half thousand vases arranged on the special tables, waiting for the final committee.

The early morning edition of the *Daily Mail* contained an advance report. The flowers sent in from

the South of England, it said, were of excellent quality. An extraordinary number of very fine blooms had come from Yorkshire. Other exceptional entries were received from Reading, Wolverhampton, Ireland, and the Channel Islands. There was no mention of Scotland.

The members of the final committee, who now arrived fresh on the scene at the Crystal Palace, consisted of ten acknowledged experts. Their examination was precise and detailed. They scrutinised not the bunch, but each individual spray. They worked in pairs, gradually accumulating on an adjacent table the one thousand and three best vases. Nine hundred bronze medals. One hundred silver medals. And three prizes.

During the course of the morning, the Countess of Bective, the appointed referee, made her entrance.

The judges worked on. It was now a question of separating nine hundred from a thousand and three.

This took time. Once again, the qualities of every spray were noted and marked. Freshness. Number of flowers on stem. Length of stem. Arrangement of flowers on stem. Size of bloom. Colour-blending.

At last it was done. The nine hundred bronze medals had been decided.

One hundred and three vases now stood alone. From these the hundred silver medallists had to be chosen. (The sun, by this time, was blazing down outside, and the Main Hall was growing oppressively hot. The shade temperature that day was to reach 88.) But even at this stage the ten experienced judges did not hurry. It was getting on towards noon, at which hour the prizes were to be announced, before they unanimously agreed on the hundred bunches which were to be awarded silver medals.

And now, separated from the rest, and placed on a table by themselves, were the three remaining bunches.

The three best. The final appraisement began.

It didn't take them very long to decide the award of third prize. Now it was a question of deciding the first. Spray by spray, stalk by stalk, bloom by bloom, the two last bunches were exactingly compared. There was argument and discussion. Some favoured the one, some the other. The minutes ticked on.

To break the deadlock, they put it to a vote. And on the count, there was a clear majority. Dutifully, the judges conveyed their decision to the referee.

At precisely twelve o'clock noon, on Friday, July 28th, 1911, the Countess of Bective stepped forward and tied the appropriate tickets to the three bunches.

Third . . . .

Second . . . .

First.

It was all over.

MIMA'S DAY

In Sprouston, at precisely noon on Friday, July 28th, Mr Fraser was sitting upstairs in his study. Mrs Fraser was busy about the house. Mima Ross was ensconced in the post-office opposite the back gate.

About half an hour later Mr Fraser was still in the study; Mrs Fraser had come upstairs, with the baby's feeding bottle, to the bedroom next door. It was another glorious summer day, and everything was quiet.

And then, in the dim interior of the tiny post-office,

the A B C Telegraph Machine gave its warning signal. Mima went to it, got out her pencil, returned the signal. Presently the pointer on the dial began to swing. Letter by letter, Mima copied down the message.

It wasn't until she was transcribing the telegram on to a form, separating it into words . . . that she suddenly grasped what it meant.

Snatching an orange envelope, she folded the form inside. Then, clutching her long skirt at the knee with one hand, and holding the envelope in the other, she ran out into the sunshine, across the road, through the back gate of the Manse, crying out for all to hear, 'He's won! He's won! *He's won!*'

Into the kitchen she dashed and thrust the telegram into the hand of the maid. The girl tore through the green baize door into the hall, up the curving staircase, burst into the study, handed the envelope to her master—and suddenly overcome by the dizziness of the moment, sank to the floor at his feet.

Attracted by the commotion, Mrs Fraser fortun-ately appeared and began to render first aid.

Calmly, Mr Fraser opened the envelope, unfolded the form, and if Mrs Fraser hadn't been attending to the girl she surely would have noticed his smile. For he had known very well, you see, which of the two bunches he sent was the better one. No, Mima hadn't got it quite right. It wasn't *he* who had won. The first prize of £1000 in the *Daily Mail* Sweet Pea Competition had been awarded to Mrs J. H. Fraser.

And that wasn't the end of it. Twenty minutes later Mima hurried across with the second telegram. This one said that the third prize of £50 had been won by the Reverend D. D. Fraser.

Out of 38,000 entries to the competition, two of the prizes had gone to the garden of Sprouston Manse.

The following morning, Saturday, July 29th, it was in the *Daily Mail*. "SCOTTISH LADY'S VICTORY" said the headline. And then, lower down, Mr Fraser's full name as the winner of the £50 prize. After that came a detailed report which described the scrupulous fairness and methodical precision with which the judging at the Crystal Palace had been conducted; how every entry in the Main Hall was repeatedly examined and assessed; the sorting and re-sorting of the special table blooms to establish the medal-winners; and the astonishment of the judges when, with the final decisions made, the names were at last revealed, and it was found that two of the prize-winning bunches had come from the same garden.

That Saturday was a day the village of Sprouston still remembers. As the news spread from mouth to mouth, Mima's telegraph receiver never seemed to stop ringing and swinging with the messages of congratulation that kept streaming in. The first arrivals were the *Daily Mail* reporters, who had travelled up by the night train to Carlisle, and then made the complicated cross-country railway journey, with all its changes, by Hawick, St Boswells and Kelso, to the tidy flower-bedecked station at Sprouston. They brought a camera and tripod with them to photograph the two prize-winners and the garden where the sweet peas had been grown. You can still see some of the pictures they took, rather faded now, in the July 31st edition of the 1911 file in London.

When it came to interviewing, the reporters caused

some slight embarrassment by innocently taking it for granted, despite the family clause in the conditions, that Mrs Fraser was an expert gardener. But the air of shyness with which the £1000 prize-winner tactfully referred their more technical questions to her knowledgeable husband was politely and no doubt gratefully accepted. Visitors arrived too that Saturday to see the Manse garden for themselves and perhaps to be given, as many were, a few sprays of Sprouston sweet peas to take home. But at last, after Mr Fraser had wound up the day's proceedings with a few touching words of thanks: after a cheer for the winners had been raised and warmly re-echoed, the visitors and reporters departed, and the young minister and his wife managed to slip away for a peaceful drive together along the quiet country roads.

A VILLAGE CHURCH

In our own time, of course, Sprouston has changed. The roads have been widened to let the traffic hurry through. Mima's shop has long since been pulled down. The Manse, with its garden, has been sold and given a different name. No parish minister lives in Sprouston now.

But there are still people in the village, or near by, who can remember the events of that famous summer of 1911, or perhaps have heard them described by their elders. They will tell you how Mima ran across with the telegram; how Alec, who was generously rewarded for his part in the success, would repeat, in his eighties, word for word what he and Mr Fraser said to each other about the sweet peas.

In their late years, Mr and Mrs Fraser, when asked about those distant days, never forgot to mention how lucky it was that the rain came to the Border Country in that vital third week of July. 'Just a coincidence, of course,' Mrs Fraser used to say. And the meteorological records certainly confirm, coincidence or not, that over the whole of the southern half of Great Britain the long drought of 1911 did not break until the day of the final judging was over.

One of the photographs the reporters took, Mrs Fraser recalled, was to show her standing beside the thirteen-foot high sweet peas, grasping a piece of foliage in one hand, and flourishing a large pair of garden scissors in the other. With a bright smile, as the picture was being taken, she smartly snapped the scissors together. Whereupon her husband, who was standing modestly in the background, advanced to whisper in her ear, 'I think I ought to tell you, my dear, you've just cut through the main shoot!'

And, yes, the house was furnished. And in 1912 the chancel was built. So if you ever find yourself passing through the village, and care to stop for a moment, perhaps there will be someone there to point out the simple white gravestone in the churchyard, and to let you into the church itself. Once inside, if you stand at the inner doorway, you'll be able to see, at the far end, the chancel with its curving arch, the two steps leading up, the stained-glass window.

Who knows? You might even see, below the window, neatly arranged in that shining vase, on the oak table, a bunch of sweet peas.

POSTSCRIPT

The writer gratefully acknowledges, in establishing the facts of the preceding narrative, the help received from staff-members of the National Library of Scotland, the Edinburgh Central Library, the Meteorological Office (Scotland), the Royal Scottish Museum, the Kelso Chronicle, and the London Office of the Daily Mail. *A complete microfilm file of the* Daily Mail *for the relevant months of the year 1911 was kindly supplied by the British Library.*

Thanks are also due to the many friends and relations of Mr and Mrs Fraser, too numerous to mention individually, who supplied background information, summoned from the past the gist of conversations, or produced letters written at the time of the events described. The parish records of Sprouston Church were made available by the Scottish Record Office, while the recollections of Miss Jemima Ross of Sprouston, of Alec White of Heiton, and Charles W. J. Unwin of Histon, Cambridge—willingly imparted either by word of mouth or by letter—made possible the detailed reconstruction of actions and scenes.

No dialogue has been invented. The words which the persons of the story are represented as uttering have been set down as Mr and Mrs Fraser, in the writer's presence, recalled and phrased them.

H.D.

GROWING SWEET PEAS

Sowing indoors; from January to March.
Fill pots with moist compost; plant seeds
3/4" deep.

Place in a warm but airy position and
keep moist. Pinch
out seedling tops
when they have
2 or 3 leaves.

Accustom
the plants
gradually to outside
conditions and plant
out from April onwards.

Sowing outdoors:
from March to
May in prepared
seedbeds ¾"
deep and 3 - 4
inches apart.

Support plants with
brushwood or netting
4 - 6 feet high.

Cut flowers regularly
and remove faded
blooms to prolong flowering.

First published in 1988
Reprinted 1995 by Canongate Books Ltd,
14 High Street, Edinburgh EH1 1TE

© text 1988 Henry Donald
© illustrations 1988 Ann Ross Paterson

A CIP catalogue record for this title is available
from the British Library

ISBN 0-86241-170-X

Printed and bound in Great Britain by BPC Paulton Books Ltd